Love
and
distance

To order additional copies of this book, please contact:
Palibrio LLC
1663 Liberty Drive
Suite 200
Bloomington, IN 47403
Toll Free from the U.S.A 877.407.5847
Toll Free from Mexico 01.800.288.2243
Toll Free from Spain 900.866.949
From other International locations +1.812.671.9757
Fax: 01.812.355.1576
orders@palibrio.com
641595

Sweetheart, from the moment I wake up here,

My heart wishes to dream of you.

Here I am, still thinking about the day when I can be together with you,

I'm still here, and the days drag on as I long to feel your warmth.

All alone here, I feel a profound pain in my bosom.

I saw a rose that was sad because it wanted to be held by you,

I saw an enamored hummingbird tasting the nectar of this flower,

I saw its madness, I saw its passion, I saw its joy, I saw its nobility,

I saw with clarity the flower's dewy tears, I saw the withered flower,

I saw how its little leaves said, "I want to hug you, my sweet heart,"

I saw how its thorns pricked its tender little heart for love,

I saw how its red color attracted its beloved,

I saw how the enamored hummingbird with its wounded wings

Tried to fly.

And lastly I saw that the wind wouldn't let it get to its tender, beautiful flower.

People tell me that I seem like a statue,

That my eyes don't blink, that sadness is abundant in me,

That I never enjoy a single moment of happiness.

Who, but who wouldn't feel that way, being in love but not having their loved one

At their side, who could feel happy?

Who would laugh? Who wouldn't feel down and unhappy? Who, I ask?

Only someone who feels no love and lives only for himself.

December is coming; the snow is coming where you are.

A blizzard is coming, the shivering cold is coming, our anniversary is coming,

The day of our first kiss of love is coming,

The passion that has been going on for 28 years to the present is coming,

The day when I took your hand is coming, the day when I put on a ring is coming,

The day when I showed you that I wanted to stay by your side is coming,

December is coming and I'm not there with you.

It seems like clear waters that are dark,

What we've had seems like an affair,

It seems like a honeycomb with no honey, it seems like a flower that never produces its fruit,

It seems like an eternal drought, this life of mine seems like breath with no air,

Not being by your side seems like a profound anguish,

It seems like being hungry and not having any food.

It seems like a cloud-flecked sky, it seems like it's raining down rocks on you,

It seems like an affliction, it seems like a mountain of eternal ailments,,

It seems like your absence is destroying my heart.

I already feel happier, I'm counting down the days to my reunion with you.

Finally, the day is within sight, the day when I'll be together with you.

The day of my renewal, the day to end the long night,

The day full of joy, the day of your unending presence,

The day in which your absence from me is ended.

You breathed new life into me, you drove away my frustration,

You gave me rest, you destroyed my desperation

You wiped away my nightmares,

You allowed a sprouting seed to live,

You took away all of my disappointments,

You harvested the reasons that bind me to you.

8

I take pencil and paper, I take a paintbrush,

I gather the paints so that not a single color is missing,

I paint and draw your face, my love.

The canvas reflects beautiful flowers which I place in your hands,

Roses, carnations. And I pour a select fragrance into the paint,

I draw your smile, your happiness, I draw your hands and mine,

I draw the light that is reflected, I draw the rivers of happiness,

In my imagination I draw my desire to be by your side.

Over there where you are, even though you're far away from me,

I know that your mind will have a place for me there, even though I'm not with you

I have your warmth if I feel cold, and there are also the sweet dreams that you've had,

The beautiful moments when you were by my side,

Over there, only over there, is where I want to be; I want to kiss you, I want to look at you,

I want to enjoy your company over there, only over there where you are.

Love is planting a seed, watering it, seeing it sprout,

It's seeing it grow with the desire to have it bear fruit. Love is wanting to be nourished

The way a hummingbird is nourished by the nectar of a flower; it's like the morning, like sunbeams,

It's like the thirst of a person who has no water. Love is cultivating affection for someone you want to get to know,

Love is fighting for the one you want to have.

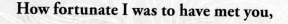

How fortunate I was to have met you,

My beloved; I feel like I'm your friend

And I have a place in your heart. I feel like the flames of love

Keep getting stronger in my life; everything I see reminds me of you.

I see a cloud, and it transforms into you. I see the stars, and they reflect the light in your eyes,

And when I go to a garden in the morning, I smell your aroma.

I see the sand, and your name and mine are there.

As for the air, what can I say? When I feel it blow across my ears

I feel like it's telling me that you love me, and as it flies away from me,

It carries my voice to you, saying that I love you, too.

12

Last night I had a dream; I dreamt that I sent myself to you in a letter in an envelope.

I dreamt that I was tiny, so very small.

But when I arrived, you didn't see me.

I called out to you, but you didn't hear me; I had to go in through one of the pores on your skin.

When I got to your heart, the door opened without my so much as touching it.

I entered there; everything was very pretty; there was a casket

Full of sweet memories; there were several photos of me, roses, songs, and poems.

I knew then that you loved me!

And how overjoyed I was! I realized that you were in love.

And when your heart beat, it made me feel very happy,

Because that told me that you love me. I didn't want to leave your heart

Alas! I awakened from my dream.

But even in my waking hours I still dream of you, my love!

13

The light came out when I met you,

The dawn awakened. There was darkness but

Even though God was with his creation, there were storm clouds.

All the other creations noticed it. The Moon, the stars.

Nevertheless, it shines forth

When a shooting star gives it what it needs to sparkle,

It gives it the energy that it needs to shine

And thus everything plays its part. The flowers have their colors, fruit has its flavor

And the sky has its marvelous blue color.

14

My butterfly

Soon you will fly here; the garden will be blossoming.

And even if you try the nectar from all of these flowers,

You won't be satisfied. However, if you kiss the lips of the gardener

Who cultivated all of this for you, you'll taste a nectar that flowers cannot give,

That only his love for you can produce.

15

My love, you feel sad and I feel sad,

You cry and I also cry, you suffer and I also suffer,

But remember that even though were far apart

We love each other. Some people are together but don't know how to love each other,

Some people are full of honey and others are full of bitterness; some light and others darkness,

Some are full of sweet dreams and others are full of nightmares.

Some people are like a flower and others are like a butterfly.

But my love is full of roses that I give to you.

You are my nectar, my aroma, my dove that will fly to me, you are my heart, my river of hope because I'm dying for you.

I have loved you in the past, I love you now, and I always will love you. Don't be sad. Be happy.

16

If I feel lonely, it's because you're not here,

That's why when I go to bed I take my pillow and give it a hug

Thinking of you. To feel your lips,

I press mine against a strawberry, in the middle of the night

So that your brown eyes will watch over my sleep.

17

My princess, your castle is very far away, and I cannot travel there,

My heart beats strongly because I cannot gaze upon you, I cannot see you

Much to my lamentation. Not being able to kiss you or touch you makes me sigh.

I feel like I can't breathe; my heart is paralyzed.

Please, I need your warmth, I feel like I'm freezing,

I'm so cold. Just come to me, my love, embrace me, come and kiss me,

So I can sleep soundly and put an end to my madness.

I'm glad that you have me beneath your roof,

Parents of my beloved, because

You let a butterfly go from a faraway garden

To another faraway land where it found a thirsty lily.

It needed someone to kiss it to open its petals.

You gave it your love in the shadow of your wings

I saw all of your faces, you sent me other nectars,

You sent me honey. My petals began to unfold.

Your love cannot dry up, rather it causes a garden to bloom.

Like a caterpillar, you let this love grow until it transformed into what it is.

You let its rose petals be our bed,

You made us feel comfortable, you protected us from sickness

By giving us your support.

May your love continue to bear such fruit so that there will always be more seeds!

19

Another day goes by and I can't touch you.

My house feels empty because you're not here.

All I know is that when you were here, everything was beautiful. Being close to you

Made me sleep easily at night. You relaxed me and when I was hot

Your breeze refreshed me. Your words were like honey from a honeycomb

And when your sweet lips kissed me, my heart beat

Faster than normal, When I woke up I was so happy that it wasn't just a dream!

You really were by my side! But now everything is cloudy

Because you're not here with me.

Now even when I want to sleep, I can't; I have insomnia because you're not here.

I wish I could sleep soundly and then wake up

With you by my side. The sky won't be cloudy anymore,

Your sunshine will keep that from happening.

Birds great and small will all sing a warbled song

And a beautiful rainbow will appear, meaning that I no longer see in black and white,

I can see blue, the color that represents love

That's what I feel for you.

I love you, honey.

My heart beats for you,

I can see the lines of your face in my mind,

The caresses of your kisses are on my lips.

My ears hear you whispering, "I love you" to me

And my face feels the tenderness of your hands.

Your passion for me captivates me,

It makes me smile, it makes me daydream.

It makes me feel happy because our love grew like

Trees grow, just like the

Gardens that bloomed. That's why my hummingbird beak

Wanted to taste the nectar of your rose blossom.

The days drag on, all I know is that I want to have you with me now.

My drought was my thirst for you. My love, my hope, and my affection for you

Reminded me of the day when we met,

My love survives the winter, summer, autumn, and spring,

My heart feels content because it will always be with you.

But I was happier when our hands were united

In the bonds of matrimony. When our lips kissed.

Just like a ship anchored in the deep, your love penetrated the very fiber of my being.

And just like the sound of the waves, my heart beat for you.

23

My tears are bitter

But my feelings are sweet,

Like waves, my eyes close and open. I feel sad, and I sigh.

All the beauty of the depths of the ocean are reflected in my eyes:

The fish, the corals, the beautiful treasures found in the depths.

But it's not difficult to get there.

Because my springs gush forth and make my feelings for you rise up.

My waters are clear but reflect blue. Like the sound of the waves

My heart beats for you.

If you look into my eyes, you'll see a beautiful landscape,

And above all, the brilliance of the sun reflecting,

You'll see seagulls flying and feeding on love instead of fish,

Because material food is soon expelled,

But the food of my heart is a passion that continues longingly,

Whoever eats it becomes hungry,

It gives them an appetite to become little fish who only want to swim.

And like an octopus, love grabs hold of you and doesn't want to let go.

24

As a fish is hooked with bait,

So is a loving kiss.

I stay on your comforting lips,

But it isn't harmful; it's a relief from the pain,

It's life, nourishment, passion, smiling, and hope,

It's what keeps you going.

Everything seems so quiet.

The cloudy horizon shows no sign of birds to sing their songs,

There's not so much as a gentle breeze.

An absolute paralysis has stricken the plants, and there aren't even any eagles flying overhead.

A faded color descends and on the dull green of the plants

Not even the moon wants to drip her dew.

Oh, nature, what has happened to you?

Hide your sadness, burn it, nourish yourself with a beautiful color.

Let the light fill your heart with a powerful whirlwind,

Let the rain and the dew fall upon you.

Let your soul be filled with joy when the sun returns

And let your lips be brushed with sweetness

Your lips that are so bitter.

26

Another night, weeks, months, minutes, and seconds

Pass by without having you by my side,

Another dark and gloomy night

During which I'm still in love, I sing, I write,

I send letters, I write poems.

Like every day for someone who suffers in the hot weather,

Its oppressive heat, like the taste of the ocean, like hurricanes,

Like being in an arid desert without any water to drink,

Like a ship anchored to the deep,

Like a storm in the ocean,

Like a well with no water,

Like being in darkness without being able to touch you or hug you,

Or kiss you, or enjoy your smile,

Or look into your eyes,

Or have your tender hands caress my face

Oh, my love!

27

You are the flower that gives nectar to my existence, you are the dew that makes

My lips thirsty for your love.

You show your true colors when you smile at me

And you cure me with your honey because I'm lovesick for you.

I want to be pollen and make you blossom so

That every bee will comment on how beautiful the garden is.

So that they will pollinate other flowers so that their sprouts will open.

So that their gardener feels happy.

28

My friends ask me why my face is obscured by a fog,

Why I don't laugh with them,

Why my spring doesn't flow.

Why my soul doesn't flourish,

Why I don't enjoy their companionship.

I tell them, if the sky lost its color,

If you couldn't taste the flavor of what you
wanted to eat,

If you couldn't smell the fragrance of your
flower,

You would realize that you missed the dawn.

Not only that, you would miss its Light,
as well as its warmth.

Because only its radiance removes you from the dense darkness.

29

Oh, my love,

I feel your absence, all I know is that your presence satisfies gives me satisfaction.

I feel depressed; I want to sleep but my eyes won't close.

Even if my eyelids lock shut like a door, even so

I can see you in my mind, and my soul laments because you aren't here.

It feels afflicted and empty, my heart stops pumping, it is weak,

It feels sad but it is also strong enough to overcome.

To wait for you and to be able to see your beauty,

To see my sadness turn into happiness.

I wish I could stay sound asleep, to stay in a dreamless sleep.

Because I don't want to wake up without you, my love.

Light entered through the window,

And the song of the mockingbird was heard.

As well as all of the animals of the mountain,

The sounds of the grasshoppers that chirp
unceasingly.

My heart starts to jump, it trembles, and is filled
with pain,

My tears of painful anguish pour down like rain.

The fear of your absence turns into lightning.

I want to sleep—No!

Better yet, I want you to be here. When I wake up

I want you to be by my side, my love!

31

I feel different from when I was a child,

Because when I was a child all I wanted was to play,

I loved my toys.

However, that love ceased to exist.

Now that I've grown up, I've fallen in love with a love that I know.

This love that I feel gets more intense,

I am captivated by its splendor,

By its affection, by its passion.

To love is better than to have toys!

My love, I see bright stars fly and how they go to where your star is.

I see the evening, I see the twilight,

I see the moon and I see its sad eyes.

So that the dew is formed

So as not to harm the cultivated flowers of the gardener

Who doesn't see the rain descend.

I see the spring, summer, autumn, and winter descend.

I've seen apple trees shed their leaves, flower, and produce.

But I haven't had an appetite for their fruit.

If their flavor was like your lips,

Then great would be my eagerness,

My desire to be filled. I want you to together with you,

I want to share my light with you, I want you to shed your woman's light on me.

I don't want the seasons to pass by as we grow apart, my love!

I miss everything about you: your body, hugging you, kissing you.

And your enchanting feminine words

That captivate your lover, that say, "I love you."

They touch your heart. It makes emotion make you feel flattered.

You feel passionate with your sweetness because it makes bitterness go

By the wayside. They remove hunger from the hungry because she wants to feed you with love.

A man feels happy with a woman like that!

34

Flames of love make me feel inspired about you, they make a fire of love relate my afflictions

And they also impassion me to become a poet for you.

Please, my love, don't stop reading these poems

Until I get to where you are.

Because then you won't have just a book, but your very own writer.

Because everything that I feel for you will spring forth out of my heart.

35

Vanessa, your name is famous and has many beautiful meanings,

It signifies the fragrance of roses, and like that fragrance, this letter is for you.

I haven't been able to go to you, my love.

How I long to be by your side!

Like a plant wants rain, so do I need you.

These days seem to drag on forever.

How miserable it is to be far from the one you love.

Our feelings have become so strong that you can't hold back the tears.

The pain in our hearts is so profound that it seems like an intense drought,

It seems like the plants will never flower and their leaves will stay dry.

Oh, my love! How I long to be by your side.

Like the great hunger that people feel, like children you who cry and their mothers, too

Because they have nothing to feed them.

My love! Forgive my handwriting, but my hands are trembling. Please

Also forgive the stains on the paper, they are from the tears that I shed because I can't be with you.

I sigh and moan from the pain.

36

Oh, my love! When will I be there with you? Time passes on, and I don't know.

How strong are my sighs, how great is my affliction.

I can't take it anymore, my hands can't even hold the pen that I'm writing to you with.

All I can tell you is that I wrote these poems for you.

Enjoy them, my love, because they tell you about my kisses,

As well as my affection and everything that I feel for you.

Take all my kisses and receive my affection, because I'm writing to you with the earnestness

Of a child.

I LOVE YOU! FROM YOUR SWEET HEART, JOSE CARLOS.

37

There are so many things that I want to talk to you about, there are so many things that

I want to tell you, there are so many things that draw me to you.

I long to kiss you and to continuously show you that I'm in love with you.

38

I get up early and my strong desire is to always

Be close to you. I wake up thinking about you and those beautiful moments

When we first met, in those days when we began our Friendship.

39

I don't know what to do anymore, distance separates us.

The days keep passing, and they seem longer than they really are,

I don't know what to do with my heart.

My strong desire for you is getting desperate,

I will keep waiting, I beg God for patience.

So that my soul will not become restless.

It will be calm until we are together again.

40

I thirst but not for water, I thirst for you.

I hunger for your kisses and hugs,

To have you here with me,

To walk with you and hold hands with you.

41

My mind feels at ease,

My soul feels at peace.

Those bitter days have passed, those dark nights

Without the shining of the moon or the light from the sun, because you are here.

42

I often dream of being by your side.

I hope to pour my passion all over you,

Fill you with joy and

Share my profound and sincere words with you that are

Meant not to hurt you but rather to assure you

That I love you a lot.

43

I never tire of telling you that I love you.

I never tire of telling you, my love.

I wouldn't stop, neither for gold nor silver,

Nor for diamonds, nor for corals, nor for precious stones.

Nor for valuable gems, because I love you deeply.

44

I ask you to forgive me if I hurt you and to console me in my affliction.

If I hurt your lips by kissing you too much. And receiving your Consolation

Because I greatly desire to have you hug me and tell me

That you need me and that you forgive me if I hurt you.

45

Beautiful rose, petals of love, your thorns are in my heart.

Your thorns don't hurt, they symbolize your buried love,

It penetrates my soul and brings me to your passion,

Meeting you was the most beautiful thing that has ever happened to me.

46

The sea erased the marks that I made when I wrote your name and mine.

But they were never erased in my heart

Which renews their memory from day to day

Because I love you. I need your affection, I need your love

Because your sunshine is my sweet reflection.

47

Now I feel sad because you have to leave.

Your kisses, your face, and your body are going away,

But what will remain is the memory of having you with me

And of having shared my love with you

Because I love you.

48

How fortunate I was to have met you, my beloved.

My love does not feel wounded, but rather content because I was able to be with you.

I touched your hands, I kissed your face, but I didn't kiss your lips

Because I have a profound respect for you.

I will only kiss them when I marry you.

49

There are many things and much joy

In knowing that I will find your unchanging love, your unchanging affection,

Your unchanging sweetness, your unchanging tenderness,

Every time you keep

Confirming that you love me.

You know, my love, that when I met you I learned a lot from you.

I learned to trust you, I learned from your tastes,

I learned from your patience,

I learned that in absence one must be patient in order to survive.

I learned to trust in God and ask him for patience and to ask him not to prolong

Your absence from me.

51

This morning has been heartbreaking for me,

It has been painful because I'm not with you.

But my love is as intense as the first day.

When I speak of heartbreak I mean that I miss you, I love you.

Above all, I want to be by your side

And to enjoy your kisses that give me life,

Air to breathe, light, color,

And my appetite. In sum, everything, because I really miss you!